The Super Fun
Joke Book

Ivy Finnegan

ARCTURUS

ARCTURUS

This edition published in 2021 by Arcturus Publishing Limited
26/27 Bickels Yard, 151–153 Bermondsey Street,
London SE1 3HA

Author: Ivy Finnegan
Illustrator: Ana Bermejo
Editor: Donna Gregory
Designer: Marie Everitt
Editorial Manager: Joe Harris

ISBN: 978-1-83940-843-4
CH008349NT
Supplier 29, Date 0321, Print run 10902

Printed in China

Contents

CHAPTER 1

Family Funnies

Why wouldn't the oyster twins share?

 Because they were two shellfish!

What did the lion cub say to its mother?

Every day I love you roar and roar!

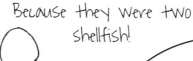

Pears!

Kurt: What has four legs, spots, and smells bad?

Bert: Me and my brother!

What happened when Granny Smith married Mr. Braeburn?

They all lived appley ever after.

What makes your brother so dumb?

He tried to borrow Facebook from the library!

WHEN ARE BASKETBALL PLAYERS LIKE BABIES?

When they dribble!

Why shouldn't you worry if you see mice in your home?

They're probably doing the mousework!

Dad: Why didn't you come straight home from school?

Sebastian: Because we live around the corner!

Frankie: There are only two things stopping me from getting onto the school soccer team.

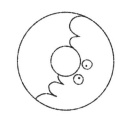

Dad: What are they?

Frankie: My feet!

Teacher: What is the plural of baby?
Frances: Twins!

WHAT CLOTHES DOES A HOUSE WEAR?

Address!

Raquel: Why does your mother wear two sweaters for golf?

Michelle: In case she gets a hole in one!

Christine: My dad can juggle eggshells, yesterday's newspaper, and an empty box!

Eugene: That's garbage!

How many kids does it take to change a light bulb?

Three—one to say, "But I didn't leave it on," and two to say, "But I changed it last time!"

What Ancient Greek land is like your brother's bedroom?

Mess-opotamia!

Where can you take a pet cat for a day trip?

To the mew-seum!

Casey: Why is your sister so good at sport?

Stacey: She has athlete's foot!

RON: WHY ARE YOU TAKING PLANKS AND A HAMMER TO THE SPORTS HALL?

John: I'm going for fencing lessons!

DAD: WHAT SHADE IS YOUR NEW CHEERLEADING UNIFORM?

Lucy: Yeller!

Why are grandpa's teeth like stars?
Because they come out at night!

My sister is so dumb, she went to the dentist to get her Bluetooth fixed!

What dog does Dracula keep as a pet?

A bloodhound!

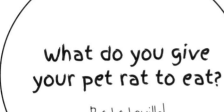

what do you give
your pet rat to eat?

Ratatouille!

CARRIE: DID YOU JUST FEED GARLIC BREAD TO OUR DOG?

Harry: Yes—its bark is much worse than its bite!

What's the difference between a boring parent and a boring book?

You can shut the book up!

DAD: WHY DID YOU OVERSLEEP THIS MORNING?

Toby: I was dreaming about a soccer game, and it went into extra time!

Why did grandma run around her bed?

She wanted to catch up on her sleep!

Karen: I wish your choir would only sing Christmas carols.

Aaron: Aw, thanks. Do you like me singing them most of all?

Karen: No, but I would only have to hear you sing once a year!

Matthew: I just banged my head on my desk.

Teacher: Have you seen the school nurse?

Matthew: No, just stars.

Charlie: Did you hear about the explosion at the French cheese factory?

Carly: Yes, all that was left was de Brie!

winnie: Why is there a plane outside your bedroom door?

Vinnie: I must have left the landing light on!

Chloe: How come you're so good at tennis?

Zoe: It's not racket science!

BOBBY: WHAT POSITION DOES YOUR BROTHER PLAY ON THE TEAM?

Robbie: I think he's one of the drawbacks!

WHICH RELATIVE VISITS ASTRONAUTS IN OUTER SPACE?

Auntie Gravity!

What did the burglar's
daughter play with
at bathtime?

A robber ducky!

My cousin is so dumb, he took
his computer to the nurse
because it had a virus!

Why was the
little iceberg just
like his dad?

Because he was a
chip off the cold
block!

Why do dogs bury bones in the ground?

Because you can't bury them in trees!

What did the mother cow say to her calf?

"It's pasture bedtime!"

WHAT IS STRANGER THAN SEEING A CAT FISH?

Seeing a goldfish bowl!

What do you give to a baby rat?

A rattle!

Nick: My dad had to go to court for stealing a calendar.

Rick: What happened?

Nick: He got twelve months!

My brother is so dumb, he went looking for a hilly lake so he could water ski!

TEACHER: WHAT'S A COMPUTER BYTE?

Samantha: I didn't even know that it had teeth!

Little sister: Why is our goldfish orange?

Big brother: Because the water makes it rusty!

What do cats eat on hot days?

Mice-cream cones!

Mother: You shouldn't play ball today, son, you have a sickness bug.

Jim: I know, I keep throwing up!

What did the father broom say to his son?

It's time to go to sweep!

WHAT CAN YOU GIVE AND KEEP AT THE SAME TIME?

A cold!

My brother is so dumb, he drinks hot chocolate at night so he will have sweet dreams!

Tilly: My aunt has one leg longer than the other.

Billy: Is she called Eileen?

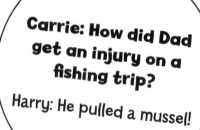

WHAT'S THE DIFFERENCE BETWEEN A HILL AND A PILL?

A hill is hard to get up, but a pill is hard to get down.

Carrie: How did Dad get an injury on a fishing trip?

Harry: He pulled a mussel!

DAD: YOU'VE BEEN WALKING SIDEWAYS EVER SINCE YOU CAME HOME FROM THE HOSPITAL.

Hannah: They said my medicine might have side effects ...

Dad, I can't mow the lawn today, I've twisted my ankle.

That's a lame excuse!

What is it called when your pet cat wins a dog show?

A cat-astrophe!

Why was the youngest of seven children late for school?

Because the alarm was set for six!

Doctor, my brother thinks he's an escalator.

Tell him to come and see me.

I can't, he doesn't go up to this floor.

Why did dad take his razor to the running track?

He wanted to shave a few seconds off his time!

EMILY: DAD, I GOT AN A IN SPELLING!

Dad: You fool, there isn't an A in Spelling!

Teacher: Did your mother help you with your homework?

Charlie: No, I got it wrong all by myself!

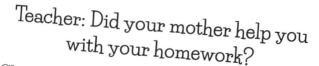

Why did Grandpa put wheels on his rocking chair?

He wanted to rock and roll!

What kind of teacher enjoys morning roll call?

The kind that keeps forgetting names!

HOW DID THE FRENCH FRIES GET ENGAGED?

With an onion ring!

What kind of monster lives in your brother's room?

The Loch Mess Monster!

WHY DID THE HOUSE GO TO THE EMERGENCY ROOM?

Because it had a window pane!

Why are cats so good at exams?

They give purrfect answers!

Mrs. Shark: What book are you studying at school, dear?

Little Shark: Huckleberry Fin!

WHAT DO YOU CALL A BABY SKUNK?

A little squirt!

Why was the frog worried about her son?

Because he looked unhoppy!

Dad: There's a burglar downstairs eating the cake your sister baked.

Ahmed: Should I call the police or an ambulance?

Sean: Why does your dog wear gloves?

Vaughn: It's a boxer!

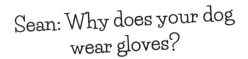

WHY DID THE JOGGER EAT ON THE RUN?

She loved fast food!

Ted: My brother got really knocked around in his last boxing match.

Ned: Sore loser?

How do you stop a rabbit from looking untidy?

Use a hare brush!

Did you hear about the cat that swallowed a ball of yarn?

She had mittens!

What do you get if you cross an owl with an oyster?

Pearls of wisdom!

What does a skeleton say to its pet dog?

"Bone appetite!"

What do you do if your pet mouse falls in the sink?

Give it mouse-to-mouse resuscitation!

WHAT KIND OF PIZZA DO DOGS ORDER?

Pupperoni!

What did the father elephant say to his kids when they weren't behaving?

Tusk, tusk.

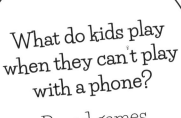

What do kids play when they can't play with a phone?

Bored games.

WHAT DO YOU DO IF YOUR COUSIN ROLLS THEIR EYES AT YOU?

Roll them back.

Why did the daddy rabbit go to the barber?

He had a lot of little hares.

Why did the God of Thunder need to stretch his muscles so much when he was a kid?

He was a little Thor.

WHAT EVENT DO SPIDERS LOVE TO ATTEND?

Webbings.

What social media app does Thanos use to talk to his friends?

Snap chat.

Do you know how many famous men and women were born on your birthday?

None, only babies.

Stacey: I was given x-rays by my dentist yesterday.

Casey: Oh, tooth pics?

Kate: Our mother is excellent at history but an awful cook.

Nate: I know, she's an expert on ancient grease!

MY BROTHER IS SO DUMB, HE FOUND THREE MILK CARTONS IN A FIELD AND THOUGHT IT WAS A COW'S NEST!

How did the shellfish know his kids were sick?

They felt clammy!

HOW DO CATS KNOW WHAT IS GOING ON IN THE WORLD?

They read the mewspaper!

Why was the sea creature worried about her son?

Because he was a crazy, mixed-up squid!

Annie: Your aunt looks so old!

Danny: Yes, she's an aunt-ique!

what do you get if you cross Dad's socks with a boomerang?

A nasty smell that keeps coming back!

Grandma: I hear you've been missing Sunday school?

Jasmine: That's a lie. I haven't missed it one bit!

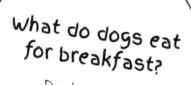

What do dogs eat for breakfast?

Pooched eggs!

What do you get if you cross baked beans with onions?

Tear gas!

WHY ARE THERE MORE GHOST CATS THAN GHOST DOGS?

Because every cat has nine lives!

WHY DIDN'T THE CAMELS GO ON A DATE?

They couldn't find a baby-spitter!

What dressing do you put on a simple salad?

Crude oil!

My sister is so dumb, she thought Spotify was a stain remover!

What happened to the man who plugged his electric blanket into the toaster?

He kept popping out of bed all night!

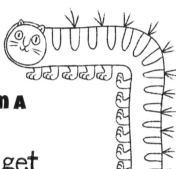

DAD, I KEEP THINKING I'M A WOODWORM!

Well, son, life does get boring sometimes!

My brother is so dumb, he thinks gluteus maximus is a Roman emperor!

Kim: Why is your drawing of a fish so tiny?

Tim: I've drawn it to scale!

Jan: How can you fit twenty friends in your room at once and still play a game?

Stan: We're playing squash!

Did you hear about the guppy that went to Hollywood?

It became a starfish!

WHEN DOES A PET CAT GO "moo?"

When it is learning a new language!

Did you hear about the embarrassing twins in the long distance race?

One ran in short bursts, the other ran in burst shorts!

Why was the baby panda so spoiled?

Because its parents panda-d to its every whim!

Did you hear that Uncle Bob lost his wig on the roller coaster?

It was a hair-raising ride!

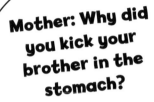

Mother: Why did you kick your brother in the stomach?

Sally: It was an accident—he turned around!

Katy: Dad, how can I join the police?

Dad: Handcuff them all together!

WHY DO LITTLE KIDS LISTEN TO THE RADIO ON LONG TRIPS?

Because car-toons keep them happy!

Grandma: What do you want to be when you grow up, dear?

Nathaniel: I'm aspirin' to be a pharmacist!

JOSIE: MY SINGING TUTOR SAID MY VOICE IS HEAVENLY!

Rosie: Not really—she said it was like nothing on Earth!

Chris: My dad's an undertaker.

Fliss: Does he enjoy it?

Chris: Of corpse he does!

Dad: What happened to your amazing five-day diet?

Edward: I finished all the food in two days!

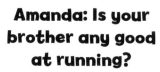

Amanda: Is your brother any good at running?

Miranda: He's so slow he ran a bath and came second!

WHAT'S THE DIFFERENCE BETWEEN AN ANGRY RABBIT AND A FORGED BANKNOTE?

One is a mad bunny, and the other is bad money!

What has a bottom at the top?

The toilet!

DEAN: CAN WE WATCH *THE CURSE OF THE BLACK PEARL* TONIGHT?

Jean: Dad won't let us watch pirate DVDs.

Mickey: Our mother has named us all after members of our family.

Nicky: Is that why your big brother is called Uncle Joe?

Edwin: I don't like cheese with holes!

Dad: Well, eat the cheese and leave the holes on the side of your plate.

My cousin is so dumb, he went to buy some camouflage pants but couldn't find any!

HOW DO YOU MAKE ANTIFREEZE?

Hide her coat and gloves!

Why was the little broom late for school?

It overswept!

Little pencil: You look as though you've put on weight, dad.

Daddy pencil: You're very blunt!

Did you hear about the magician who tried his sawing-a-person-in-two tricks at home?

He had lots of half brothers and sisters!

Clark: Why is your grandpa
dressed as a clown?

Mark: Jest for fun!

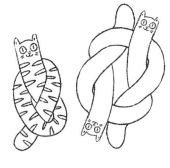

**Why was the baby
strawberry crying?**

Because her mother and father
were in a jam.

Matt: Why did
your dad quit
his job at the can
crushing plant?

Kat: Because it was
soda pressing!

**GRAN: WHY ARE YOU EATING THAT
BAGUETTE IN THE BATHTUB?**

Stan: It's a sub sandwich!

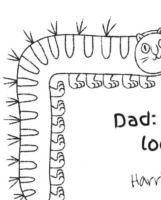

Dad: Why do your shoes look like bananas?

Harriet: They're my slippers!

What did the mother dog say to her puppy?

"We're having dinner soon, don't eat too much homework!"

WHY DO RATS HAVE LONG TAILS?

Because they'd look silly with long hair!

What do you get if you cross a cocker spaniel, a poodle, and a rooster?

Cockerpoodledoo!

WHAT HAPPENED TO THE DOG THAT SWALLOWED A FIREFLY?

It barked with de-light!

What did the little corn say to the mama corn?

Where is pop corn?

Mother: What do IDK, LY, and TTYL mean?

Daughter: I don't know, love you, talk to you later.

Mother: Well, I'll have to ask your sister then!

Ned: Why is the light always on in your brother's room?

Fred: Because he's so dim!

Florence: Why do you only play baseball at night?

I have a vampire bat!

Flo: Why are you crying and chewing at the same time?

Joe: I just swallowed some blubber gum!

WHAT DO YOU GET IF YOU CROSS A DOG AND A FROG?

A pet that can lick you from the other side of the road!

DAD: HAVE YOU HAD YOUR HOMEWORK MARKED YET?

Becky: YeS, I'm afraid you didn't do very well!

Why did the girl stare at the carton of orange juice?

It said "concentrate."

Alan: Is my supper ready? I have karate class in an hour.

Mother: Your chops are on the table!

Why can't you hear a psychiatrist go to the bathroom?

Because the P is silent!

Drew: If can't is short for cannot, what is don't short for?

Sue: Donut?

Why are cats so good at playing the piano?

Because they are very mew-sical!

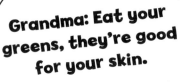

Grandma: Eat your greens, they're good for your skin.

Alice: But I don't want green skin!

WHO ARE SMALL, FURRY, AND FANTASTIC AT SWORD FIGHTING?

The three mouseketeers!

WHAT DO A PET DOG AND A PHONE HAVE IN COMMON?

They both have collar ID!

My sister is so dumb, she thought goosebumps were to stop geese from speeding!

Thelma: If that planet is Mars, what's the one higher up?

Velma: Is it Pa's?

Fred: My teacher says I should train to be an astronaut.

Jed: No, she said you're a real space cadet ...

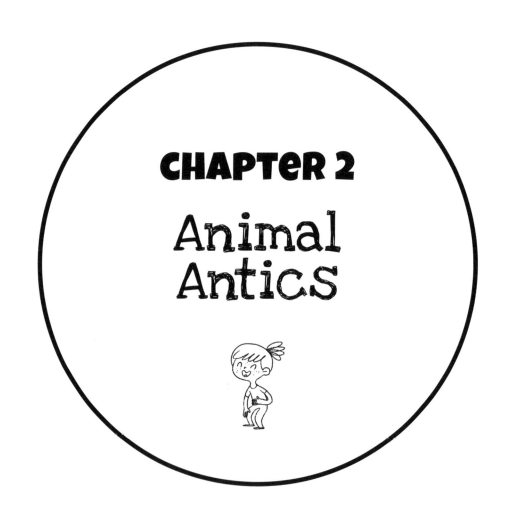

CHAPTER 2

Animal Antics

Cindy: Did you know it's raining cats and dogs out there?

Mindy: I know, I just stepped in a poodle!

What's the difference between weather and climate?

You can't weather a tree, but you can climate!

Why do fish in a school all swim in the same direction?

They're playing Salmon Says!

WHAT IS IN THE MIDDLE OF A JELLYFISH?

Its jellybutton!

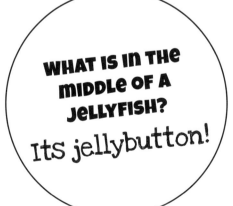

WHAT DID THE COW SAY WHEN IT WAS HUNGRY?

"Thistle have to do!"

Why do male deer need braces?

Because they have buck teeth!

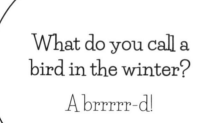

What do you call a bird in the winter?

A brrrrr-d!

why is it hard to wind up a snake?

You can't pull its leg!

Why are frogs always happy?

Because they can eat whatever bugs them!

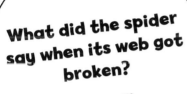

What did the spider say when its web got broken?

"Darn it!"

Why did the shark bang its head against the bottom of the ship?

It was a hammerhead!

WHAT DID ONE RAINDROP SAY TO THE OTHER?

"Two's company, three's a cloud!"

WHAT DO YOU CALL A MAN WITH A SEAGULL ON HIS HEAD?

Cliff!

What did the insect say before it tried a bungee jump?

Earwig-o!

What do you call a woman who is good at fishing?

Annette!

When should a mouse stay indoors?

When it's raining cats and dogs!

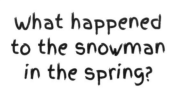

What happened to the snowman in the spring?

He made a pool of himself!

Why don't whales watch sad movies?

It makes them blubber!

Doctor, I keep thinking that I'm a dog!

Climb up on the couch, and I'll take a look at you.

But I'm not allowed on the couch!

WHAT DID THE CRAB SAY TO HER GROUCHY HUSBAND?

"Don't get snappy with me!"

What's the difference between a storm and a horse?

One is reined up and the other rains down!

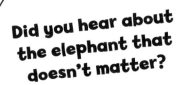

Did you hear about the elephant that doesn't matter?

It's an irrelephant.

WHAT DOES A BUILDER USE TO FIX THE APE HOUSE AT THE ZOO?

A monkey wrench!

Did you hear about the hippo at the North Pole?

It got hippothermia!

WHY DO DIVERS APPROACH OCTOPUSES VERY CAREFULLY?

Because they're heavily armed!

How do you describe an acorn?

In a nutshell, it's an oak tree!

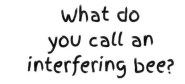

What do you call an interfering bee?

A buzzybody!

What do you call an ant from overseas?

Import-ant!

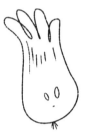

Why was the zebra put in charge of the army?

Because he had the most stripes.

What ice-cream does a gorilla like best?

Chocolate chimp.

WHAT DO YOU GET IF YOU CROSS A DINOSAUR WITH A FISH?

Jurassic shark.

What did the polar bear say to the melting ice?

"You need to cool down!"

**Which animals
were last to leave
Noah's Ark?**

The elephants, because
they had to pack
their trunks.

Why wasn't the octopus
afraid of being attacked?

It was well armed!

What do you call a bear
with no teeth?

A gummy bear.

HOW CAN YOU TELL IF A CAT LIKES THE RAIN?

Because when it rains, it purrs!

Why do elephants paint their toenails red?

So they can hide in cherry trees.

What do you call a woman with a cat on her head?

Kitty.

WHERE DO RABBITS LEARN TO FLY?

In the Hare Force!

What has big ears, four legs, and a trunk?

A mouse with its luggage.

Which bird is always out of breath?

A puffin.

How do you wake
up a llama?

With a llama clock.

Why are dogs such bad dancers?

They have two left feet.

**HOW DO YOU
GET AROUND ON
THE SEABED?**

By taxi-crab.

Why don't dolphins play poker for money?

Because of all the card sharks!

Why are fish so clever?

They swim in schools!

Why wouldn't the crab twins share their rock pool?

Because they're two shellfish!

WHAT IS A GOOD PET FOR BABIES?

A rattlesnake.

What's the difference between a storm cloud and a bear raiding a beehive?

One pours with rain and the other roars with pain!

what do you call a baby crab?

A little nipper!

Where do saplings go to learn?

Elemen-tree school!

WHAT TYPE OF DOG CAN TELL THE TIME?

A watchdog.

WHY DID THE LION SPIT OUT THE CLOWN?

Because he tasted funny.

What do you get when you cross a parrot and a cat?

A carrot.

What sport do horses like best?

Stable tennis.

Which cats are great at bowling?

Alley cats.

How do you stop a dog from barking in the back seat of a car?

Put it in the front seat.

What did the tiger eat after he'd had all his teeth pulled out?

The dentist.

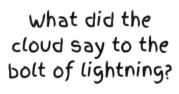

What did the cloud say to the bolt of lightning?

"You're shocking!"

WHY DO WHALES SING?

Because they can't talk!

What game do elephants like to play?

Squash.

WHAT'S RED AND GREEN AND JUMPS OUT OF PLANES?

A parrot-trooper.

What kind of bird does construction work?

A crane.

What did the short-sighted porcupine say to the cactus?

"Ah, there you are, Dad!"

HOW DO YOU GET IN TOUCH WITH A FISH?

You drop it a line!

Why did the vultures argue?

They had a bone to pick with each other!

What lives in the forest and repeats itself?

A wild boar.

How does a fish save its money?

It goes to the riverbank!

What does an octopus wear in the winter?

A coat of arms.

WHAT SORT OF HORSES DO GOBLINS RIDE?

Night mares.

Why did the cat pounce on the computer?

Because he saw a mouse.

Why did the hippo go to the doctor?

It was a hippochondriac!

What's worse than
raining cats and dogs?

Hailing taxis!

What do you call a man who lives
wild with a pack of wolves?

Wolfgang!

What do you call a hippo at the South Pole?

Lost!

WHAT DO YOU CALL A GIRL WITH A SHEEP ON HER HEAD?

Barbara!

Why did the firefly keep crashing?

He wasn't very bright.

What do you call an alligator who's a thief?

A crookadile.

What do you get if you cross a tarantula with a rose?

We're not sure, but don't try smelling it!

DID YOU HEAR ABOUT THE SNAKES THAT ARGUED?

They agreed to hiss and make up!

What do you call an alligator private eye?

An investi-gator.

WHY DID THE LEOPARD REFUSE TO TAKE A BATH?

Because he didn't want to become spotless.

What's worse than a crocodile with a toothache?

A centipede with athlete's foot.

Why didn't anyone laugh at the farmer's jokes?

They were too corny!

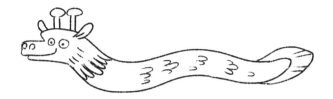

WHAT IS THE SADDEST CREATURE IN THE OCEAN?

Why does a frog have more lives than a cat?

Because it croaks every night.

The blue whale!

How do elephants travel long distances?

In jumbo jets.

Can you name five animals found at the North Pole?

Four seals and a polar bear!

Why did the elephant refuse to play cards with his two friends?

Because one was a lion and the other was a cheetah!

WHERE DO YOU BUY BABY BIRDS?
At the chickout.

What do you call rabbits marching backward?

A receding hare-line.

Do fish like to watch baseball?

Yes—there are 20,000 leagues under the sea!

Why was the pig covered in ink?

Because it lived in a pen.

WHY COULDN'T THE SNAKE SAY ANYTHING?

It had a frog in its throat!

What do you call a prisoner's canary?

A jail bird.

What do you call a cat with eight legs?

An octopuss.

What do you call a hamster who can pick up an elephant?

Sir!

What do you give a sick parakeet?

Tweetment.

Did you hear about the snake that was trying to impress its date?

It was a snake charmer!

WHAT DO ELEPHANTS DO WHEN IT RAINS?

They get wet!

What did one flea say to the other flea?
"Should we walk or take the dog?"

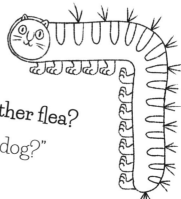

WHEN DO MONKEYS FALL FROM THE SKY?

During Ape-ril Showers!

What did the bird say as it finished building its nest?

"That's the last straw!"

Why shouldn't you be mean to a butterfly?

Because you might hurt its feelers!

DID YOU HEAR THAT DOROTHY AND TOTO GOT CAUGHT IN A STORM?

It was the Blizzard of Oz!

What are little
sea creatures
most afraid of?

Squid-nappers!

What do you
call a bear in wet
weather?

A drizzly bear!

Why did the owl 'owl?

Because the woodpecker would
peck 'er!

Why don't owls date in thunderstorms?

It's too wet to woo!

Why are mosquitoes religious?

Because they're always preying on something!

WHAT DO YOU CALL A DEAD FLY?

A flew!

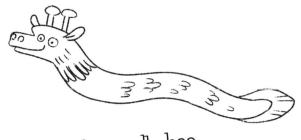

What gift did the smelly bee receive from its friends?

Bee-odorant!

WHY DID THE SICKLY CRAB WALK SIDEWAYS?

Its medicine had side effects!

what did the worm say to her son when he came home late?

"Where in earth have you been?"

Did you hear about the cow that was blown away by a tornado?

It was an udder disaster!

What's the largest moth in the world?

A mammoth!

What do you call a fly with no wings?

A walk!

PHIL: IS IT GOING TO RAIN TODAY?

Bill: I drought it!

Why are spiders like wheels?

Because they are good at spinning!

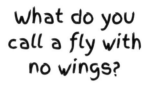

WHAT DO YOU CALL A SLEEPING BULL?

A bull-dozer.

What goes snap, crackle, pop?

A firefly with a short circuit!

How do you fit more pigs on your farm?

Build a sty-scraper!

How do bees celebrate moving to a new place?

With a house-swarming party!

WHAT SOUND DO PORCUPINES MAKE WHEN THEY HUG?

Ouch!

why are teddy bears never hungry?

They are always stuffed!

Why do gorillas have big nostrils?

Because they have big fingers!

Where do polar bears vote?

The North Poll.

What do you get from a pampered cow?
Spoiled milk!

Why did the snake cross the road?

To get to the other sssssssssside!

What fish only swims at night?

A starfish!

HOW DOES A LION GREET THE OTHER ANIMALS AT THE WATER-HOLE?

Pleased to eat you.

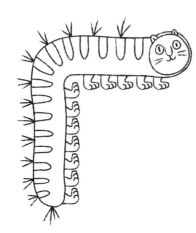

Why didn't the ranger believe the tiger?

He thought it was a lion!

WHAT DO YOU GET WHEN YOU CROSS A SNAKE AND A PIE?

A pie-thon!

What is "out of bounds?"

An exhausted kangaroo!

Why are cats so good at video games?

Because they have nine lives.

what did the buffalo say to her son when she went away for a work trip?

Bison!

How do bees get to school?

By school buzz!

Why did the turkey cross the road?

To prove he wasn't chicken!

WHAT ANIMALS ARE ON LEGAL DOCUMENTS?

Seals!

what do you get if you cross fireworks with a duck?

A firequacker!

Why can't a leopard hide?

Because she's always spotted!

Why did the pony have to gargle?

Because it was a little horse!

HOW DO CHICKENS BAKE A CAKE?

From scratch!

WHAT SONG DOES A CAT LIKE BEST?

Three Blind Mice.

How do prawns and clams communicate?

With shell-phones!

Why do dogs run in circles?

Because its hard to run in squares!

How do pigs write secret messages?

With invisible oink!

What's the difference between a guitar and a fish?

You can tune a guitar, but you can't tuna fish.

Which kind of horse can jump higher than a house?

All of them—houses can't jump!

Why do cows wear bells?

Because their horns don't work!

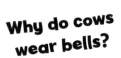

WHERE DO SHEEP GO ON HOLIDAY?

To the Baaaaaa-hamas!

WHAT KIND OF MONKEY FLIES THROUGH THE AIR?

A hot air baboon!

What's the most dangerous flower in the garden?

A tiger lily!

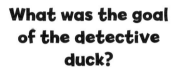

What was the goal of the detective duck?

To quack the case

What did the teacher say when the horse walked into the class?

Why the long face?

What do you get if you cross a pig with a dinosaur?

Jurassic Pork!

What is beautiful, has big ears, and wears glass slippers?

Cinderelephant!

How do bees brush their hair?

With a honeycomb!

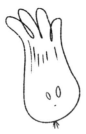

WHY DO HUMMINGBIRDS HUM?

Because they forgot the words!

Why are cats scared of trees?

Because of their bark.

WHY DID THE FISH BLUSH?

Because it saw the ocean's bottom.

A sheep, drum, and a snake fall off a cliff.

Baa-Dum-Tsssss!!!

What kind of ties do pigs wear?

Pig sties!

Why did the horse sail on a boat?

He was in the Neigh-vy!

What do you call the cat police?

Claw Enforcement!

Where do cows go at the weekend?

To the moo-vies!

WHY DO YOU NEVER SEE ELEPHANTS HIDING IN TREES?

Because they're really good at it!

WHY DID THE PELICAN GET KICKED OUT OF THE RESTAURANT?

He had a big bill.

What's a dog's number one breakfast food?

Pooched eggs.

what do you call a monkey with a wand?

Hairy Potter!

What STEM subject are owls really good at?

Owlgebra!

CHAPTER 3

Celebration Chuckles

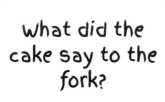

What did the cake say to the fork?

You wanna piece of me??

How does a sheep say Merry Christmas?

Fleece Navidad!

WHAT DID THE PAINTER SAY TO HER SWEETHEART?

I love you with all my art.

Why do candles always go on the top of cakes?

Because it's really hard to light them from the bottom.

what kind of cake do
ghosts like?

I Scream Cake.

What kind of candy is
never on time?

Choco-LATE.

**WHY IS IT SO COLD
AT CHRISTMAS?**

Because it's
Decembrrrr!

What do you call two birds in love?

Tweethearts!

WHAT DID THE CHRISTMAS TREE SAY TO THE DECORATIONS?

"Aren't you tired of just hanging around?"

What did the candle say to the other candle?

"I'm going out tonight!"

What did Mrs. Claus say when an elf shed a tear?

"Don't get so Santa-mental, darling!"

What goes up but never comes down?

Your age.

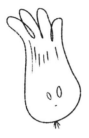

What did the loaf of bread say to the other loaf of bread during Hanukkah?

Happy challah days!

WHAT DO SNOWMEN LIKE TO DO AFTER CHRISTMAS?

Chill out!

How did Darth Vader know what Luke Skywalker was getting for his birthday?

He felt his presents.

What drink did the ghost order at the drive-through?

Boo-nana milk shake!

HOW DO PICKLES CELEBRATE THEIR BIRTHDAY?

They relish it.

What do vampires do at the end of the school year?

Blood tests!

Why was Santa's little helper so sad?

Because he had low elf esteem!

What do you call a spaceship covered in sugar and vinegar?

A sweet-and-sour saucer!

What happens if no one comes to your birthday party?

You can have your cake and eat it, too.

What kind of ball doesn't bounce?

A snowball!

WHY ARE THERE ONLY 8 DAYS OF HANUKKAH?

Because 7 ate 9.

If you have a dozen eggs in one hand and 10 cupcakes in the other, what do you have?

Crazy-big hands.

What did the turkey say when it saw the farmer?

"Quack, quack!"

What do you call someone who steals gift wrap from the rich and gives it to the poor?

Ribbon Hood!

What did the Easter bunny say to the carrot?

"It's been nice gnawing you!"

WHAT KIND OF FOOD IS SUITED TO VALENTINE'S DAY?

A hearty meal!

What did the ram write in his Valentine?

"Will ewe be mine?"

Did you hear about the tree's birthday celebration?

It was really sappy.

IF SANTA TRAVELS IN A SLEIGH, WHAT DO HIS ELVES TRAVEL IN?

A minivan!

What do birds do on Halloween?

They go trick-or-tweeting!

What do cakes and baseball teams have in common?

They both need a good batter.

What did the Cyclops write in his Valentine card?

"You're the one eye adore!"

What do mathematicians eat for Thanksgiving dinner?

Pumpkin pi!

WHY IS DRACULA SO UNPOPULAR?

Because he's a pain in the neck!

How does a lemon ask for a hug?

"Give me a squeeze!"

Did you hear about the angels that got married?

They lived harpily ever after!

WHAT DID THE NEEDLE SAY TO THE BUTTON?

"I love you sew much!"

Did you hear about the lazy skeleton?

It was bone idle!

What did Dracula say when he didn't receive any Valentines?

"This sucks!"

What did one star say to another star?

"Do you want to glow on a date?"

Why did Goldilocks fall fast asleep?

She was in the house with the three bores!

WHAT TAKEOUT DOES THE EASTER BUNNY USUALLY ORDER?

Hop Suey!

WHAT DO YOU CALL A BUNCH OF BALLOONS IN THE BATHROOM?

A birthday potty.

What did one bee say to the other?

I love bee-ing with you, honey!

Why did the robber break into the bakery?

She heard the cakes were rich.

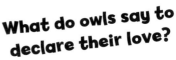

What do owls say to declare their love?

Owl be yours!

When do werewolves go trick-or-treating?

Howl-oween!

What kind of flowers should you NOT give on Valentine's Day?

Cauliflowers!

In which direction do you head to find chocolate eggs?

A little Easter here!

WHY WAS THE CHICKEN STRESSED?

Because she'd mislaid her eggs!

Why did the student eat their homework?

Because the teacher said it was a piece of cake!

What do you give to an Easter chick with a cold?

A hen-kerchief!

What do you get in December that you don't get in any other month?

The letter D!

WHAT'S RED AND WHITE, AND RED AND WHITE, AND RED AND WHITE?

Santa stuck in a revolving door!

WHAT GOES "OH, OH, OH?"

Santa walking backward!

What one thing will you get every year on your birthday, guaranteed?

A year older.

What game
do vampires love
to play?

Casketball!

Did you hear about the gullible vampire?

He was a real sucker!

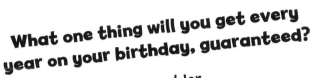

Why are Christmas trees bad at sewing?

Because they always drop their needles!

WHERE WAS THE DECLARATION OF INDEPENDENCE SIGNED?

At the bottom!

What did the one sheep say to the other?

I love ewe!

And how did the other sheep respond?

You're not so baaaaaa-d yourself

HOW DO YOU THROW A PARTY ON MARS?

You planet.

What did the cucumber say to the pickle?

You mean a great dill to me.

Why did Santa get a parking ticket?

He left his sleigh in a snow parking zone!

How did the phone propose to his girlfriend?

He gave her a ring.

What does Mrs. Claus say when she sees black clouds?

"Looks like rain, dear!"

Why does the Statue of Liberty stand for freedom?

Because she can't sit!

HOW DO YOU MAKE A TISSUE DANCE?

Put a little boogie in it.

Why is Cinderella bad at soccer?

Because she runs away from the ball.

What does Simba say to celebrate every Hanukkah?

Hanukkah matata.

WHY DID RUDOLPH HAVE A BAD GRADE ON HIS REPORT CARD?

Because he went down in history!

What does a turtle do on its birthday?

Shell-ebrates.

What's the cleanest type of birthday party joke?

One that's a soap-prise.

WHAT DID THE TWEENAGER GIVE HIS MOTHER FOR HER BIRTHDAY?

Ughs and kisses!

Why was the birthday cake so hard?

It was a marble cake!

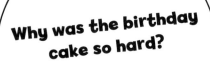

How does Santa know what presents to give each person?

He looks for the Santa clues!

What do you say to an octopus on Valentine's Day?

I want to hold your hand, hand, hand, hand, hand, hand, hand, hand!

What did the farmer give her husband for Valentine's Day?

Hogs and kisses.

WHAT DID THE CAKE SAY TO THE DONUT?

You're looking glazed over.

what do you call a ghost's true love?

His ghoul-friend.

What did one light bulb say to the other light bulb on Valentine's Day?

I wuv you watts and watts!

What should
you wear to
Thanksgiving dinner?

A har-vest!

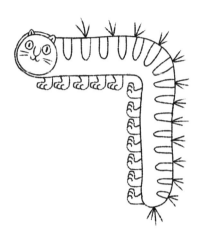

What do ghosts
put on their turkey
at Christmas?

Grave-y!

**Where do the elves
go to dance?**

A snowball!

WHAT CAN YOU SEE FLYING THROUGH
THE SKY ON CHRISTMAS EVE?

A U.F. Ho-Ho-Ho!

What did the almond say to the pistachio?

"You're nut so bad, you know!"

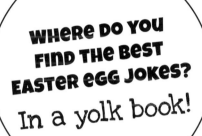

WHERE DO YOU FIND THE BEST EASTER EGG JOKES?

In a yolk book!

Who delivers presents to pets?

Santa Claws!

Who visits mermaids at Easter?

The oyster bunny!

What do you call Santa when he's asleep?

Santa Pause!

Why don't skeletons like Thanksgiving?

They haven't any body to spend it with!

WHAT TIME DO CHICKENS WAKE UP?

Six o'cluck!

what kind of music is bad for balloons?

Pop.

WHAT DID THE STAMP SAY TO THE ENVELOPE ON VALENTINE'S DAY?

I'm stuck on you!

What's the difference between a knight and Rudolf?

One slays the dragon, the other's draggin' the sleigh!

What do you get when you combine a Christmas tree with an iPad?

A pineapple!

What do you call the world's smallest Valentine's Day card?

A valen-teeny.

WHAT DID ONE SNOWMAN SAY TO THE OTHER SNOWMAN?

Do you smell carrots??

what do you write in a slug's Valentine's Day card?

Be my Valen-slime!

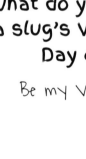

What's the best Hanukkah gift for the person who has everything?

A burglar alarm.

What did the gymnast say to her Valentine?

"I'm head over heels in love with you!"

What did the girl cat say to the boy cat?

"I think you're purr-fect!"

Why did the vampire's birthday meal give him heartburn?

Because it was a stake sandwich!

WHERE DO YOU FIND THE MOST FAMOUS MISTLETOE?

Holly-wood!

Which hand is best to light the menorah with?

Neither, it's best to light it with a candle.

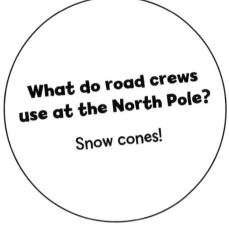

What do road crews use at the North Pole?

Snow cones!

What did the skeleton write in her Valentine card?

"I love every bone in your body!"

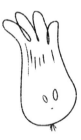

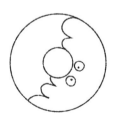

WHAT DOES SANTA WRITE ON FUNNY TEXT MESSAGES?

HHHOL!

WHAT KIND OF PHOTOS DO ELVES TAKE?

Elfies!

How did Jack Frost break his wrist?

He fell off his icicle!

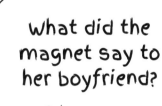

What did the magnet say to her boyfriend?

"You're very attractive!"

Why are graveyards such noisy places?

Because of all the coffin!

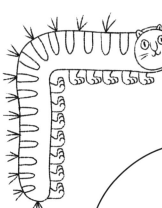

What do you call the Easter bunny if he has fleas?

Bugs Bunny!

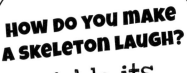

HOW DO YOU MAKE A SKELETON LAUGH?

Tickle its funny bone!

What Christmas song do they sing in the desert?

"Oh Cam-el Ye Faithful!"

What is it called if you're afraid of Christmas?

Santa Claus-trophobia!

What did the woodcutter's wife say to her husband on December 1st?

"Not many chopping days left until Christmas!"

Why did the scientist use a microscope to read his Valentine card?

Because it was Valen-tiny!

What do vampires sing on New Year's Eve?

Auld Fang Syne!

WHAT DO YOU SAY TO A RABBIT ON ITS BIRTHDAY?

Hoppy Birthday!

What's the best way to catch the Easter bunny?

Hide in a bush and make a noise like a carrot!

Where is the best place to go on Halloween?

The scream park!

Why are turkeys wiser than chickens?

Ever heard of Kentucky Fried Turkey?!

HOW DO ELVES GET TO THE TOP FLOOR?

An elf-avator!

WHEN DO GHOSTS PLAY TRICKS ON EACH OTHER?

April Ghoul's Day!

In what year does New Year's Day come before Christmas?

EVERY year!

What kind of insect hates Christmas?

A bah humbug!

What message was inside the rabbit's Valentine card?

Some bunny loves you!

What do snowmen eat for breakfast?

Frosted Flakes!

What monster plays tricks on Halloween?

Prank-enstein!

What does every birthday end with?

The letter Y.

WHAT DO YOU GET IF SANTA COMES DOWN THE CHIMNEY WHEN THE FIRE IS LIT?

Crisp Cringle!

How does Good King Wenceslas like his pizza?

Deep pan, crisp, and even!

WHAT WAS THE CHEF'S SECRET INGREDIENT FOR LOVE?

Valen-thyme!

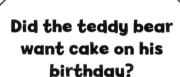

Did the teddy bear want cake on his birthday?

No, he was stuffed.

Did you hear about the couple who met in a revolving door?

They're still going around together!

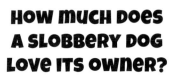

HOW MUCH DOES A SLOBBERY DOG LOVE ITS OWNER?

Drooly, madly, deeply!

What did the tiger say to her cub on his birthday?

It's roar birthday!

What does Mowgli sing at Christmas?

"Jungle Bells, Jungle Bells ..."

Why do skunks love Valentine's Day?

Because they're scent-imental!

Does a green candle burn longer than a pink one?

No, they both burn shorter.

Why did the turkey want to join a band?

Because he already had the drumsticks!

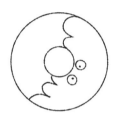

Why did the Easter bunny want to move?

He was fed up of the hole thing!

WHAT DO REINDEER HANG ON THEIR CHRISTMAS TREES?

Horn-aments!

Why did the tortoises get married?

Because they were turtle-y in love!

WHY COULDN'T THE ELF WORK IN SANTA'S TOYSHOP?

He had tinselitus!

When does Christmas come before Thanksgiving?

In the dictionary!

What food do ghosts love the most?

Ice scream!

WHICH RIDE DO GHOSTS ENJOY THE MOST?

The roller ghoster!

What did the rectangle write in the triangle's Valentine?

"I think you're acute!"

What sort of jokes do Easter chicks like?

Corny ones!

Who dresses in red and white, and is a danger in the water?

Santa Jaws!

What did the boa constrictor write in its Valentine card?

"I have a crush on you!"

DID YOU HEAR THAT THE EASTER BUNNY WON THE LOTTERY?

He's a million-hare!

Doctor, I can't sleep because i am so excited about Christmas!

Lie on the edge of your bed, and you'll soon drop off!

What song does a bull sing on Valentine's Day?

"When I fall in love ... it will be for heifer."

What sneaks around the kitchen on Christmas Eve?

Mince spies!

What do you call a vampire that eats all the time?

Snackula!

WHERE DOES A SNOWMAN KEEP HIS MONEY?

In a snow bank!

What kind of people are the best at Easter egg hunts?

Eggsplorers!

CHAPTER 4

Hysterical History

**Why did soldiers fire arrows
from the castle?**

They were trying to get their
point across!

**DID CAVE PEOPLE
HUNT BEAR?**

No, they wore
clothes!

Who succeeded
the first President
of the United
States?

The second one!

Teacher: Can you think of an ancient
musical instrument?

Jake: An Anglo-saxophone?

Who said "cluck cluck" and conquered half the world?

Attila the hen!

What do you call a frog who wants to be a cowboy?

Hoppalong Cassidy!

WHY DID THE SOLDIER PUT A TANK IN HER HOUSE?

It was a fish tank!

What happened to the royal chicken that couldn't lay eggs?

The Queen had her eggs-ecuted!

WHAT WAS ROBIN HOOD'S MOTHER CALLED?

Motherhood!

Why did the King visit the dentist?

To have his teeth crowned!

Which owl robbed the rich to give to the poor?

Robin Hoot!

What do you get if you cross a hangman and a circus performer?

Someone who goes straight for the juggler!

Why did Archaeopteryx always catch the worm?

It was an early bird!

How did Vikings send secret messages?

They used Norse code!

WHY DID THE COWBOY CHOOSE HIS HORSE IN DAYTIME?

He didn't want nightmares!

Which Russian leader was a big fan of fruit?

Peter the grape!

What did Queen Victoria say when she stepped in cow dung?

"We are not a-moo-sed!"

What did Attila the Hun and Catherine the Great have in common?

The same middle name!

Teacher: Can you tell me what nationality Napoleon was?

Fiona: Course I can!

WHO IS THE HEAD OF THE UNDERWATER CRIME RING?

The codfather!

Which book did Mark Twain enjoy writing the most?

Huckleberry Fun!

What do you call a sleeping Triceratops?

A dinosnore!

Who was the most feared gunfighter in the ocean?

Billy the Squid!

WHAT DO YOU CALL A FORTUNATE DETECTIVE?

Sheerluck Holmes!

what do kings and
queens drink?

Royal-tea!

**Which famous knight
never won a battle?**

Sir Endor!

How did Neil
Armstrong say he
was sorry?

He Apollo-gized!

WHAT DID ROBIN HOOD WEAR TO THE BALL?

A bow tie!

HOW DO YOU INTERRUPT A KNIGHT?

"Joust a minute...!"

Why was Al Capone best friends with a fisherman?

They got along by hook or by crook!

Did you hear about the timid dinosaur?

It was a nervous Rex!

In which battle was Genghis Khan killed?

His last one!

Which figure in history ate the most?

Attila the hungry!

How did King Arthur find Queen Guinevere?

He followed the foot prince!

Which fish was once the ruler of Russia?

The tsar-dine.

WHAT DO YOU CALL A FRIENDLY PHARAOH?

A chummy mummy!

Why is it no fun being an archeologist?

Their career is always in ruins!

Dawn: I wish I'd been born 500 years ago.

Shaun: Why's that?

Dawn: So I wouldn't have to learn so much history!

WHAT IS A FORUM?

Two-um plus two-um!

Which monarch had the worst skin?

Mary Queen of Spots!

WHY WAS THE PHARAOH SO TENSE?

He was getting wound up!

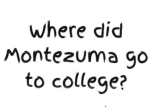

Where did Montezuma go to college?

Az Tech!

Shirley: When was the Magna Carta signed?

Hurley: 1215.
Shirley: Oh, just before lunch then!

Why did Columbus cross the ocean?

To get to the other tide.

What did Anne Boleyn's lady in waiting say on her wedding day?

"That man's not worth losing your head over!"

Where did the teacher send the Viking when he got sick in class?

To the school Norse!

WHAT DID NOAH DO FOR A LIVING?

He was an ark-itect!

Who was the first European cat to visit America?

Christofur Columpuss!

Why did the Stegosaurus need first aid?

It was dino-sore!

Why did the Pilgrims want to set sail during the spring?

Because April showers bring May flowers.

WHY DID THEY CALL KING ALFRED "THE GREAT?"

Because Alfred the fantastic sounded wrong!

What was Camelot?

A good place to park camels.

How did the Hunchback of Notre Dame cure his sore throat?

He gargoyled!

What was Queen Victoria's most treasured item of clothing?

Her reign-coat!

WHAT SWEET TREAT DID CAVE PEOPLE LIKE THE BEST?

Spearmints!

What happened when the wheel was invented?

It caused a revolution!

HOW DID EGYPTIANS BEGIN LETTERS OF COMPLAINT?

"Tomb it may concern ..."

Which gorilla had six wives?

Henry the Ape!

What invention lets you see through walls?

The window!

What do you say to get Romans to sing along?

"All toga-ether now!"

Major: I didn't see you in camouflage training this morning, Private!

Private: Thank you very much, Ma'am!

WHERE DO COWBOYS COOK THEIR MEALS?

On the range.

Which English person invented fractions?

Henry the Eighth!

Why was it hot inside the Colosseum?

Because of all the gladi-radiators!

Did you hear about the queen whose eldest son disobeyed her?

She was having a bad heir day!

Why did the pioneers cross the country in covered wagons?

Because they didn't want to wait 40 years for a train!

Which knight hid around corners to make people jump?

Sir Prise!

WHY DID ANCIENT CIVILIZATIONS HAVE NICE, SMOOTH CLOTHES?

They lived in the Iron Age!

WHAT MOVIE DID THE ANCIENT GREEKS LIKE BEST?

Troy Story!

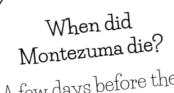

When did Montezuma die?

A few days before they buried him!

What was in fashion at the time of the Great Fire of London?

Blazers!

why were the dark ages so confusing?

It was common to hear, "Good morning, good knight!"

Who invented matches?

Some bright spark!

Why did Sir Walter Raleigh sail to South America?

It was too far to swim!

What happened when electricity was first discovered?

People got a nasty shock!

WHAT DO YOU CALL A ROMAN EMPEROR WHO HAS ADVENTURES?

An action Nero!

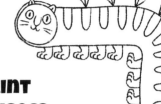

WHY DID CAVE PEOPLE PAINT PICTURES OF HIPPOPOTAMUSES?

They couldn't spell it!

Why is history such a sweet subject?

Because it's full of dates!

Why didn't George Washington bother going to bed?

Because he couldn't lie!

How do you find Tutankhamen's tomb?

Peer-amid the other tombs!

Which Roman Emperor was a practical joker?

Julius Teaser!

Why did cave people love to eat sloths?

They knew that fast food was bad for you!

Why was it called the Dark Ages?

Because there were so many knights!

WHAT WAS WRITTEN ON THE KNIGHT'S TOMB?

Rust in peace!

What was King Arthur's jester called?

Joe Kerr!

HOW WAS THE ROMAN EMPIRE DIVIDED UP?

With a pair of Caesars!

Which animal invented the internet?

The beaver, since it was the first to log on!

What was the score at the ancient Egyptian soccer game?

One-nile!

What did one Aztec say to another?

We all have to make sacrifices!

Which fruit launched a thousand ships?

Melon of Troy!

WHY WERE BRITISH PEOPLE REALLY TANNED OVER 2,000 YEARS AGO?

They lived in the Bronzed Age!

How do dinosaurs pass their exams?

With extinction!

Why did the mummy call the doctor?

Because he was coffin!

WHICH ANCIENT GREEK WAS THE BEST OF THE BUNCH?

Alexander the Grape!

Why was King Arthur's table round?

So he couldn't be cornered!

Why was the bullheaded creature
not allowed to vote?

Because it was only a minor-taur!

WHAT BUS SAILED ACROSS THE ATLANTIC?

Christopher Colum-bus!

Why did everyone in nineteenth-century England carry an umbrella?

Because Queen Victoria's reign lasted for 64 years!

Why couldn't the animals play cards
on Noah's Ark?

Because Noah was standing on the deck!

WHERE DO EGYPTIAN MUMMIES GO FOR A SWIM?

The Dead Sea!

Where did King Arthur's soldiers get their training?

Knight school!

Why does the Statue of Liberty stand in New York?

Because it can't sit down!

What did Julius Caesar say when Brutus stabbed him?

"Ouch!"

What did the executioner say to the prisoner?

"Time to head off!"

Why was Abraham Lincoln buried in Springfield, Illinois?

Because he was dead!

What's another name for the Dark Ages?

Knight time!

WHAT WAS THE FIRST THING SAID BY THE INVENTOR OF THE STINK BOMB?

"You reek, ugh!"

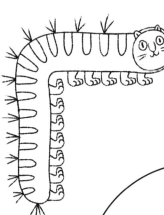

Why did the Romans build such straight roads?

So their soldiers didn't go around the bend!

Did you hear about the mummy that lost its temper?

It flipped its lid!

What did the dragon say when it saw Sir Lancelot?

"Ugh, more canned food!"

TEACHER: WHAT CAME AFTER THE STONE AGE AND THE BRONZE AGE?

Adrian: The Saus-age?

WHERE DID THE PILGRIMS LAND WHEN THEY ARRIVED IN AMERICA?

On the beach!

What music was popular with Egyptian mummies?

Wrap music!

What do you call it when the Queen goes to the bathroom?

A royal flush!

What did the colonists wear at the Boston Tea Party?

Tea-shirts!

Mr. Money: I asked my class to name a creature that was half-man and half-beast.

Mr. Honey: So did I. They said Buffalo Bill.

Which emperor should have stayed away from gunpowder?

Napoleon Blownapart!

What was Camelot famous for?

Its knight life!

WHY DID AL CAPONE FIRE HIS CLEANER?

He wanted to be a famous grime lord!

WHO RIDES A HORSE, WEARS A MASK, AND SMELLS GOOD?

The Cologne Ranger!

What was the first thing Queen Victoria did on ascending to the throne?

Sat down!

Why was Pharaoh so boastful?

He Sphinx he's the best.

How did Noah navigate in the dark?

He used floodlights!

What were the first islands
Columbus sighted?

The Aha!-mas!

What happened when they finally
got the cards on Noah's Ark?

Their game was ruined by
two cheetahs!

What did Robin
Hood say when he
nearly got shot at the
archery contest?

"That was an arrow
escape!"

WHY WERE THE ANCIENT
EGYPTIANS GOOD AT
SPYING?

They kept things
under wraps!

WHAT DOES AN EXECUTIONER READ IN THE MORNING?

The noose-paper!

What do history teachers do on a date?

Talk about the good old days!

Who designed the round table?

Sir Cumference!

What do you get if you cross a Roman Emperor with a boa constrictor?

Julius Squeezer!

What do you call a cave person who has been buried since the Stone Age?

Peat!

WHY DID THE COWBOY RIDE A HORSE?

It was too heavy to carry!

Why did Triceratops go to the playground?

It loved the dino-see-saw!

Which Roman Emperor was asthmatic?

Julius Wheezer!

Why wouldn't the ancient Egyptian accept that his boat was sinking?

He was in de-Nile!

Why did the Viking need cheering up?

He had a sinking feeling.

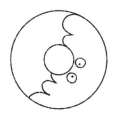

What kind of tea were the colonists looking for?

Liber-tea!

WHY DID THE ARCHER CHANGE HIS CAREER?

He found the job too arrowing!

HOW DID PEOPLE TIE THEIR SHOELACES IN THE MIDDLE AGES?

With a long bow!

What kind of music did cave people listen to?

Rock music!

Why did the soldier salute a tiger?

It had more stripes!

Who sat at the round table to write everything down?

King Author!

Nero: What time is it?

Servant: X past V!

In which part of a tomb did the ancient Egyptians bury the dead?

In the pyra-middle!

WHAT KIND OF JEWELS DID THE ANCIENT EGYPTIANS DECORATE THEIR COFFINS WITH?

Tomb-stones!

What creature hunted in prehistoric oceans?

Jurassic shark!

WHAT DINOSAUR WOULD HARRY POTTER BE?

The DinoSorcerer

When did the Vikings make their raids?

During a plunder storm!

Two wrongs don't make a right, but what do two Wrights make?

An airplane!

Why didn't the ancient Egyptians have doorbells?

They just toot-and-come-in!

Did you hear the joke about the Liberty Bell?

It cracked me up.

How did Christopher Columbus get to college?

On a scholar-ship!

What does a triceratops sit on?

Its tricera-bottom.

WHICH ROMAN EMPEROR WAS THE COOLEST?

Julius Freezer!

Which knight was King Arthur's best lookout?

Sir Veillance!

WHAT LETTERS ARE LIKE A ROMAN EMPEROR?

The "c"s are!

How did cave people dress in the snow?

Quickly!

What did the cowboy say when his dog left?

"Doggone!"

What was the name
of the inventor of
the computer?

Chip!

**DID YOU HEAR ABOUT THE
UNEMBALMED ANCIENT
EGYPTIAN DISCOVERY?**

It Sphinx!

**Why did the
hangman's wife ask
for a divorce?**

Her husband was a
pain in the neck!

What do you call a paleontologist who
sleeps all the time?

Lazy bones

CHAPTER 5

Magical Mirth

WHY WAS THE MERMAN SO CLEVER?

He was always fin-king!

How did Jack count how many beans his cow was worth?

He used a cow-culator!

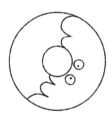

How is a Cyclops like a pig?

They both have one i in the middle!

How did the Greek god know which toothbrush to use?

The handles said, "His and Hermes!"

Why don't many people pass the test to become a witch?

Because it's very diff-occult!

What's the tale about an infected toenail?

Pus in Boots!

WHAT DID THE WITCH DO WHEN HER BROOMSTICK BROKE?

She witch-hiked!

What do you call a bowl of melted chocolate flying through space?

A flying saucer!

Did you hear about the married magicians who could make themselves invisible?

Their kids were nothing to look at either!

How many elves does it take to change a light bulb?

Ten: one to twist the bulb and nine to stand on each other's shoulders!

What do you get if you cross Cerberus and a hyena?

I don't know, but I'd join in if it laughs!

WHAT'S WOODEN, HAS A LONG NOSE, AND GOES BOING?

Pinocchio on a bungee jump!

Why did Little Miss Muffet need a map?

Because she'd lost her whey!

How does Percy Jackson contact the gods?

He calls them on the Persephone!

DID YOU HEAR ABOUT THE MAGICIAN THAT LOST HIS TEMPER ON STAGE?

He pulled his hare out!

Why do witches get stiff joints?

They suffer from broomatism!

What has a blue face and a
horn on its forehead?

A unicorn holding its breath!

**Why did Rapunzel
go wild at parties?**

She liked to let her
hair down!

Where do the
toughest dragons
come from?

Hard-boiled eggs!

**WHAT'S BROWN, FURRY, AND HAS
TWELVE LEGS?**

The Three Bears!

Who has fangs and webbed feet?

Count Quackula!

WHAT DO YOU CALL A WIZARD FROM OUTER SPACE?

A flying sorcerer!

Why did Dopey stare at the orange juice carton all day long?

Because the label said "Concentrate."

Why are mermaid's parties so popular?

Everyone has a whale of a time!

What do you call a unicorn without a horn?

Completely pointless!

WHAT DO YOU CALL AN OGRE WITH A TWISTED ANKLE?

A hobblin' goblin!

what do ghouls put on their bagels?

Scream cheese!

What did the golden snitch say when Harry Potter was bitten by a mosquito?

Quidd-itching!

What does Cinderella wear underwater?

Glass flippers!

What did Aladdin do when he lost his lamp?

He used the flashlight app on his phone instead!

What tests do teenage wizards take?

Hexaminations!

WHAT DID THE UNHAPPY GHOST SAY?

"Boo-hoo!"

What kind of music do mermaids like?

Bubble rap!

Why does Sleepy curl up in the fireplace?

He likes to sleep like a log.

WHY DO DRAGONS LAY EGGS?

Because if they dropped them, they would break!

Why can you always hear mumbling outside Jack's house?

Because Jack and the beans talk!

WHERE DO YOU FIND A GIANT SCHOLAR?

Around the neck of a giant's shirt!

What do the Greek gods drink for breakfast?

Orange Zeus!

Who told the big, bad wolf he was ugly and smelly?

Little Rude Riding Hood!

What did the werewolf say when it stubbed its toe?

Aoooooooowwwww!

What did Hansel and Gretel say when they broke the witch's house?

"That's the way the cookie crumbles!"

WHERE DO SHEEP GO FOR THEIR HAIRCUT?

Barber black Sheep!

What do you call a mermaid that speaks French?

So-fish-ticated!

Why do baby snakes stay close to their parents?

Because a boa's best friend is his smother!

Did you hear about the magician that threw his watch up in the air?

He wanted to see time fly!

Do you know the fairy tale about the Frog Prince?

Reddit ...

Why did the elf struggle to concentrate at school?

He had a short attention span!

WHY WAS HARRY POTTER GIVEN DETENTION?

He was cursing in class!

DID YOU HEAR ABOUT THE UGLY CYCLOPS?
He was a sight for a sore eye!

What's the best way to greet a werewolf?

"Howl do you do?"

Did you hear the story about a miserable bear?

It was a Grimm furry tale!

Why won't you get to the underworld on a rainy day?

Because you have to make Hades while the sun shines!

Did you hear about the magician that disappeared during his act?

He was going through a stage!

WHAT DO ELVES USE TO SERVE ICE CREAM?

A microscoop!

How should you feel if you meet a three-headed dog?

Terrier-fied!

What noise does a flying witch make?

"Brooooooooom!"

Why doesn't Harry Potter's godfather like practical jokes?

He's too Sirius!

What has sharp teeth and lives at the end of the rainbow?

The croc of gold!

HOW DID THE MERMAID TRAVEL TO THE HOSPITAL?

In a clambulance!

Why did Goldilocks stir the porridge really hard?

Because Daddy Bear told her to beat it!

Why did the pixie move out of the toadstool?

Because there wasn't mushroom.

WHICH GREAT DETECTIVE IS THREE FEET TALL AND HAS POINTED EARS?

Sherlock Gnomes.

How does an octopus make a mermaid laugh?

With ten-tickles!

What do you call a wizard on a horse?

Harry Trotter!

WHAT FRUIT DO VAMPIRES LOVE?

Neck-tarines!

What kind of spells did the whirling wizard cast?

Dizzy spells.

Why couldn't the wizard's victim move?

He was spellbound!

Where do American banshees go on school trips?

Lake Eerie!

Why don't bad-tempered witches ride broomsticks?

They're afraid of flying off the handle!

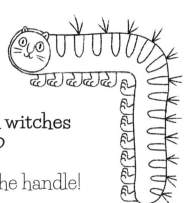

WHAT SHOULD YOU DO WITH A GREEN DRAGON?

Wait for it to ripen!

How do Death Eaters freshen their breath?

With Dementos!

What do you call a one-eyed creature on a bike?

A cycle-ops!

Why couldn't the mermaid tune in her radio?

She was on the wrong wavelength!

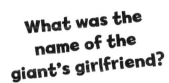

What was the name of the giant's girlfriend?

Fifi Fo-Fum!

What does a witch buy at the hairdresser's?

Scare spray!

WHAT DOES GRUMPY PACK IN HIS LUNCHBOX?

Sour grapes!

HOW CAN YOU TELL IF A BANSHEE IS POLITE?

She only shrieks when she's spoken to!

Who grants your wishes but smells of fishes?

The fairy codmother.

Did you hear the story about the Princess who drank too much juice?

It's called *The Princess and the Pee!*

What do you call a warlock who stops fights?

A peacelock.

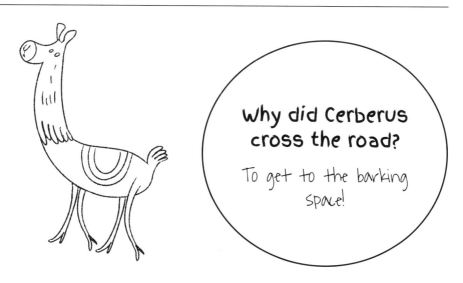

Why did Cerberus cross the road?

To get to the barking space!

What kind of breakfast cereal do they serve at hogwarts?

Hufflepuffs!

What is the difference between a dragon and a mouse?

Have you had your eyes tested recently?

**Why is Snow White kind to all
of the seven dwarfs?**

Because she's the fairest of them all.

**HOW DID JACK
BREAK INTO THE
GIANT'S CASTLE?**

Intruder
window!

What does a unicorn
call its father?

Popcorn!

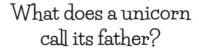

How do mermaids
make a decision?

They flipper coin!

Why did the dragon breathe on the map of the Earth?

Because she wanted to set the world on fire!

Teacher: What should you do if you find a spaceman?

Student: Park in it, man!

Why should you never trust the big bad wolf when he's in bed?

Because he's lying!

WHAT DO YOU CALL A CREATURE THAT GETS LOST WHEN THERE'S A FULL MOON?

A where-wolf!

WHAT DAY DO WEREWOLVES LIKE THE BEST?

Moon-day!

Why do witches love hotels?

They always order broom service!

Why did the Cyclops quit teaching?

Because he only had one pupil!

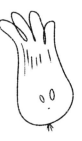

Which unicorn is always top of the class?

The A-corn!

What is higher than a giant?

A giant's hat!

What can you hear at Halloween saying, "Bite, slurp, ouch!"?

A vampire with a toothache!

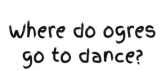

Where do ogres go to dance?

To an odd-ball!

WHAT IS INSIDE ALADDIN'S LAMP?

It would take a genie-us to know that!

HOW DOES AN OGRE CLEAN THE BATHROOM?
He uses disin-Shrek-tant!

Where does a goblin go shopping?

At the grossery store!

What do you call a nervous witch?

A twitch!

Why was Cinderella no good at sports?

Because her coach was a pumpkin!

What did the fairy call her daughter?

Wanda!

Why did the witch date an I.T. EXPERT?

She wanted to marry a computer wizard!

Why did the cuttlefish annoy the mermaid?

He was always squidding around!

WHY DIDN'T THE MERMAID BELIEVE WHAT HER FRIENDS TOLD HER?

It sounded fishy!

What do fairies use to
tie back their hair?

Rainbows!

What do you call
Quidditch players who
share a dorm?

Broom-mates!

**Have you heard the
story about a poor
little spider?**

It's called Spinderella!

**WHERE DOES CERBERUS
SIT AT THE MOVIES?**
Anywhere it likes!

WHAT DID THE MERMAID KEEP AS A PET?

A catfish!

What happened when the girl vampire met the boy vampire?

It was love at first bite!

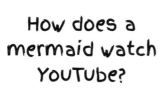

How does a
mermaid watch
YouTube?

On the Net!

If "Open Sesame" opens the cave, which
piece of treasure makes it close?

A locket!

What did the ghost write in his girlfriend's valentine card?

You're simply boo-tiful!

Which dessert makes the swamp monster lick her lips?

Key slime pie!

Why didn't the alien eat the clown?

He said it tasted funny!

WHY DO FAIRIES CARRY WANDS?

Because wands can't walk!

WHAT DO YOU GET IF YOU PUT A WIZARD AT THE NORTH POLE?

A cold spell!

Why did the ghost go up the stairs?

To raise its spirits!

What do you call a fairy that never takes a bath?

Stinkerbell!

What do you give an ogre with enormous feet?

Plenty of room!

Why couldn't the ghost find its dad?

Because he was transparent!

WHAT PROTECTS THE GROUNDS OF HOGWARTS?

De-fence against the dark arts!

How does an ogre count to twelve?

On his fingers!

How do you get Dracula's autograph?

Join his fang club!

What does a short-sighted ghost need?

Spook-tacles!

Why didn't the pixie invite his school friend for supper?

His mother couldn't stand the goblin!

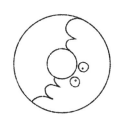

Why was the genie grumpy when he came out of his lamp?

Someone had rubbed him up the wrong way!

WHAT SPORT DO MERMAIDS AND SEAHORSES PLAY?

Water polo!

HOW MANY WIZARDS DOES IT TAKE TO CHANGE A LIGHT BULB?

It depends what you want to change it into!

What do you call a magical dog?

A labra-cadabra-dor!

What kind of stories do giants like?

Tall tales!

Did you hear about the joke they played on Humpty Dumpty?

He fell for it!

How long should an elf's legs be?

Just long enough to reach the ground!

who goes out with an ogre?

Her boy-fiend!

Why doesn't Voldemort wear glasses?

No one nose!

WHAT HAPPENED WHEN TWO BANSHEES MET EACH OTHER AT A PARTY?

It was love at first fright!

Why did Lucius Malfoy cross the road twice?

Because he was a double-crosser!

WHY DOES PETER PAN FLY EVERYWHERE?

He Neverlands!

Zeus: Has the goddess of war been here today?

Hercules: Yes, Athena a while ago.

What do you call a spaceship that doesn't mind its own business?

A prying saucer!

Do monsters eat snacks with their fingers?

No, they eat the fingers separately.

what is a vampire's best-loved sport?

Bat-minton!

Why should you never sleep with your head under the pillow?

Because the tooth fairy might take all your teeth!

HOW DO LITTLE WITCHES LISTEN TO BEDTIME STORIES?

Spellbound!

What happened to the tired fairy who lay down on a branch?

He soon dropped off!

WHAT'S THE FIRST THING A WITCH READS IN A MAGAZINE?

Her horror-scope!

Why did the mermaid blush?

Because she saw the bottom of the ocean!

Why do vampires need mouthwash?

Because they have bat breath!

WHERE DO YOU FIND GIANT SNAILS?

On a giant's fingers!

Which nursery rhyme character talks too much?

Blah blah black sheep!

What do elves learn when they start school?

Their elfabet!

Where do you find Dumbledore's Army?

Up his sleevy!

What do you call a dog magician?

A labracadabrador.

Which fish come out at night?

Starfish!

WHY IS MAD-EYE MOODY SUCH A BAD TEACHER?

He can't control his pupils!

Where do mermaids watch movies?

At the dive-in!

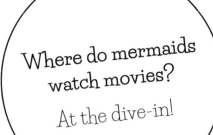

who is in charge of the lighting at Halloween?

The lights witch!

Why can't Elsa have a balloon?

Because she will let it go.

Have you heard the fairy tale about three holes in the ground?

Well, well, well!

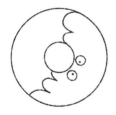

WHY DID THE WIZARD FLUNK SCHOOL?

He was terrible at spelling!

CHAPTER 6

Travel Ticklers

Why do astronauts take sandwiches on board their rocket?

They get hungry at launch time!

What has big ears, four legs, and a trunk?

A mouse with its luggage.

where do sharks go for a change of scene?

Finland!

WHAT'S IN THE MIDDLE OF AUSTRALIA?

The letter R!

Where do cows spend the night when they're away from home?

A moo-tel!

Why couldn't the farmer water her garden?

There was a leek in her bucket!

How does an astronaut get his baby to sleep?

Rocket!

WHAT DO YOU CALL A PIRATE WITH WOODEN ARMS AND LEGS?

Bob!

Why do kangaroos hate bad weather?
Because the kids have to play inside!

Did you hear about the commuter who ate gum every morning?
He caught the chew-chew train!

What are the only notes pirates can sing?
High Cs!

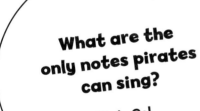

WHAT GOES MOOZ?
A spaceship reversing!

Which country is the best at the 100m sprint?

Iran!

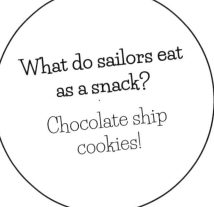

What do sailors eat as a snack?

Chocolate ship cookies!

what do you call a teddy bear that takes off its shoes and socks to paddle?

Bear-foot!

WHAT DO YOU CALL A TIGER AT THE BEACH?

Sandy Claws!

What is the biggest thing in
an American's pencil case?

Pencil-vania!

Why do sailors always
carry soap?

In case they have to wash
themselves ashore!

What do you get
if you run behind
a car?

Exhausted!

WHAT ITEM IS ALWAYS IN FASHION
FOR TRAIN DRIVERS?

Platform shoes!

Which river do snake hunters flock to?

The Hississippi!

WHAT DO YOU CALL A COUNTRY WHERE EVERYONE DRIVES A PINK CAR?

A pink car-nation!

What was the highest mountain before Everest was discovered?

Still Mount Everest!

What do you call a toy train set?

A play station!

WHEN IS A SAILOR LIKE A PLANK OF WOOD?

When he's aboard!

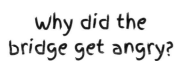
Why did the bridge get angry?

Because people were always crossing it!

What did the baby bicycle call its father?

Pop-cycle!

Where can you find an ocean without water?

On a map!

What bird is commonly found in Portugal?

Portu-geese!

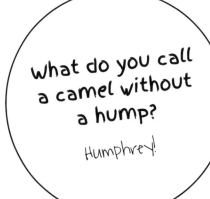

What do you call a camel without a hump?

Humphrey!

What game do astronauts play to kill the time?

Moon-opoly!

WHAT WOULD YOU GET IF YOU CROSSED A RIVER AND A DESERT?

Wet and thirsty!

How many planets are
out in space?

All of them!

WHY DID THE ROBOT GO AWAY FOR THE SUMMER?

It needed to recharge its batteries!

What do you call a Spanish man who can't find his car?

Carlos!

Why do ghosts visit the same
places on every trip?

They like their old haunts best!

which capital city is growing at the fastest rate?

Dublin!

What is the best day to go to the beach?

Sunday!

WHAT DID THE BREAD DO ON ITS LUNCH BREAK?

Just loafed around!

Why did the spy get arrested at the station?

She was trying to cover her tracks!

What stays in the corner yet can travel all over the world?

A stamp.

What's purple and fishy and found off the coast of Australia?

The Grape Barrier Reef!

Why did the emu cross the road?

To prove it wasn't chicken!

WHICH IS THE MOST POLITE TOURIST ATTRACTION IN THE WORLD?

The Leaning Tower of Please-a!

Where should a dog never go shopping?

A flea market.

WHAT'S BROWN, HAIRY, AND WEARS SUNGLASSES?

A coconut at the beach!

What do you call a French man wearing sandals?

Phillipe Flop!

Why won't you starve if you get shipwrecked by a beach?

You can eat all the sand which is there!

What's the best day for
a sailing trip?

Winds-day!

WHAT'S SMALL, FURRY, AND PURPLE?

A koala holding its breath!

Did you hear about the pig that went on a plane?

Swine flu!

Where is Hadrian's Wall?

Around Hadrian's garden!

Which animal was the first in space?

The cow who jumped over the Moon!

Why do bananas use sunscreen?

Because they peel!

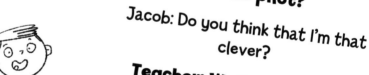

Teacher: Have you considered a career as an airline pilot?

Jacob: Do you think that I'm that clever?

Teacher: Well, you always have your head in the clouds!

WHAT IS THE FASTEST COUNTRY IN THE WORLD?

RuSha!

WHERE DO EGGS GO FOR A WEEKEND BREAK?

New Yolk!

What's the best thing to do on a trip to the Arctic?

Just chill.

Why don't elephants travel by train?

They don't like putting their trunks on the luggage rack!

What did the cruise liner say as it sailed into port?

"What's up, dock?"

Did you hear about the cuddly sea captain?

She liked to hug the shore!

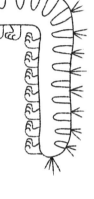

What did one mountain say to the other?

"You're looking a little peaky!"

WHICH SIDE OF A PORCUPINE IS THE PRICKLIEST?

The outside!

How do you get to see a school of fish?

Travel by octobus!

WHAT STEPS SHOULD YOU TAKE IF YOU SEE AN ALIEN?

Large ones!

Why did the pirate visit the computer store?

To buy an iPatch!

What do you say to a frog that is hitching a ride?

"Hop in!"

What's the best car for driving through water?

A ford!

What did the Pacific Ocean say to the Atlantic Ocean?

Nothing, it just waved!

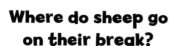

Where do sheep go on their break?

The baa-haa-maas!

Why couldn't the astronaut book a hotel on the moon?

Because it was full.

What did Tennessee?

The same thing Arkan-saw!

Why should you go on a scuba-diving trip?

Just for the halibut!

What do clowns wear to go swimming?

Giggles!

WHY SHOULD YOU AVOID FRUITCAKE WHEN YOU'RE ON A BOAT?

It may contain dangerous currants!

What did the Italian say when she returned from an overseas trip?

"Rome, sweet Rome!"

WHAT FAMOUS PORTUGESE CITY DO SKELETONS LIKE TO VISIT?

Lis-bone!

What kind of witch likes the beach?

A SAND-witch.

Which country's people have the nicest teeth?

Brussia!

What do you call a country populated only by donkeys?

An assassination!

WHY IS IT HARD TO FIND A CAMEL IN THE DESERT?

Because they're well camel-flaged!

What's big, white, furry, and always points North?

A polar bearing!

How did the cyclist get a puncture?

She didn't see the fork in the road!

What falls at the North Pole but never gets hurt?

Snow!

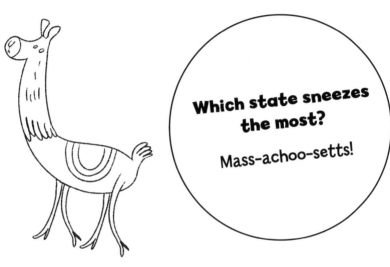

Which state sneezes the most?

Mass-achoo-setts!

Why did the octopus travel to space?

To visit the Galack-Sea!

WHAT ROCK GROUP HAS FOUR men WHO DON'T SING?

Mount Rushmore!

Where do LEGO people go
on holiday?

The Czech Repu-brick!

**WHAT'S THE
COLDEST COUNTRY?**

Chile!

How do
mountains see?

They peak!

What do they sing on your birthday in Iceland?

"Freeze a jolly good fellow!"

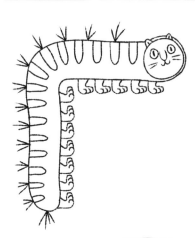

Where do penguins go to vote?

The South Poll!

Which country is the slippiest?

Greece!

WHY SHOULD YOU NEVER ARGUE ON A HOT-AIR BALLOON RIDE?

You don't want to fall out!

How do you cut the sea in half?

With a see-saw.

CAN YOU NAME FIVE ANIMALS FOUND AT THE NORTH POLE?

"Four seals and a polar bear?"

What's the best thing about Switzerland?

I don't know, but the flag is a big plus!

What do you call the little rivers that flow into the Nile?

Juveniles!

What's the smallest state in the US?

Mini-sota!

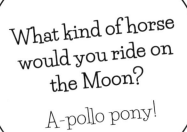

What kind of horse would you ride on the Moon?

A-pollo pony!

Did you hear about the frog that parked illegally?

It got toad away!

WHY WOULD YOU TAKE A BASEBALL GLOVE ON A SURFING TRIP?

So you can catch a wave!

HOW DO LIGHTHOUSE KEEPERS COMMUNICATE WITH EACH OTHER?

With shine language!

What do you need to drive your car along the beach?

Four-eel drive!

What keeps on running without getting tired?

A river!

What has big ears, four legs, and two trunks?

An elephant with spare parts!

Why did the polar bear cross the road?

To go with the floe!

WHAT DO YOU CALL A LAZY BABY KANGAROO?

A pouch potato!

What did one beach say to the other beach?

"Show me your mussels!"

What do you think of that new diner on the moon?

The food was good, but there really wasn't much atmosphere.

WHAT HAPPENS WHEN YOU WEAR A WATCH ON A PLANE?

Time flies!

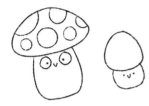

What do you get when you cross a plane with a magician?

A flying sorcerer!

What kind of tree fits in your hand?

A palm tree!

Why was the librarian denied permission to board the plane?

Because it was overbooked!

Why do the French love to eat snails?

They don't like fast food!

What do Inuit people use to hold their houses together?

Iglue!

WHERE CAN YOU FIND THE ANDES?

At the end of your armies!

Why can't a bicycle stand up on its own?

Because it's two tired!

What are microwaves?

They're what fleas surf on!

WHERE DO HAMSTERS GO ON THEIR HOLIDAYS?

To Hamsterdam!

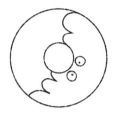

What do you call a Great Dane wearing a snorkel?

Scuba-Doo!

What did E.T's mother say to him when he got home?

Where on earth have you been?!

Which country is the spiciest?

Chile!

What do you call a boomerang that doesn't come back?

A stick!

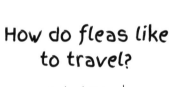

How do fleas like to travel?

Itch hiking!

WHY ARE MOUNTAINS THE FUNNIEST PLACE TO TRAVEL TO?

Because they're hill areas!

what do you get if you cross a kangaroo and an elephant?

Great big holes all over Australia!

WHAT COUNTRY HAS THE MOST GERMS?

Germany!

Where is a teacher's top vacation spot?

Times Square!

Where do pepperonis go on holiday?

The Leaning Tower Of Pizza!

WHERE DO BEES GO ON THEIR HOLIDAY?

Stingapore!

Why did the witch stay in a hotel?

Because she heard they had great broom service!

Which Canadian city is a favorite vacation spot for American trees?

Montreeal

What's the best kind of sandwich for the beach?

Peanut butter and jellyfish.

WHAT GOES THROUGH TOWNS, UP HILLS, AND DOWN HILLS BUT never moves?

The road!

What do frogs eat in the summer?

Hopsicles!

Why does a seagull fly over the sea?

Because if it flew over the bay, it would be a baygull.

What did the kid say when her teacher told her she'd missed summer school?

"No, Sir. I didn't miss it at all."

WHAT'S WORSE THAN A CROCODILE CHASING YOUR SAFARI GROUP?

Two crocodiles chasing your safari group.

why do fish swim in saltwater?

Because pepper water would make them sneeze!

What has a nose and flies but can't smell?

A plane!

Why did the starfish blush?
Because the sea weed.

What's black and white
and red all over?

A zebra with a sunburn!

What do astronauts wear
when they aren't in their
space suits?

Apollo shirts!

**What is yellow and
dangerous?**

Shark-infested
custard!

WHAT DO YOU CALL A DROID THAT TAKES THE LONG WAY AROUND?

R2 detour.

What injections does an astronaut have before a trip?

Booster shots!

HOW CAN YOU TELL THAT THE OCEAN IS FRIENDLY?

It waves!

How does the sun drink water?

Out of sunglasses!

How does a pirate travel when he's on land?

By carrrrrrr!

WHAT DO YOU GET IF YOU COMBINE A FISH WITH AN ELEPHANT?

Swimming trunks!

What do you call a stranded polar bear?

Ice-olated!

Where would you visit to see a man-eating fish?

A seafood restaurant!

What do you get if you meet a shark in the Arctic Ocean?

Frostbite!

What does a cloud wear under
his raincoat?

Thunderwear.

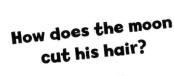

How does the moon
cut his hair?

Eclipse it.

**WHAT SHOULD YOU
TAKE TO AVOID
SEASICKNESS?**

Vitamin Sea!

What is big, furry, and
flies?

A hot-air baboon!